THE GLENS OF ANTRIM

STEVEN HANNA

HALSGROVE

First published in Great Britain in 2010

British Library Cataloguing-in-Publication Data
A CIP record for this title is available from the British Library

ISBN 978 1 84114 953 0

HALSGROVE
Halsgrove House,
Ryelands Industrial Estate,
Bagley Road, Wellington, Somerset TA21 9PZ
Tel: 01823 653777   Fax: 01823 216796
email: sales@halsgrove.com

Part of the Halsgrove group of companies
Information on all Halsgrove titles is available at: www.halsgrove.com

Printed in China by SNP Leefung Printers Ltd

INTRODUCTION

How can you sum up the Glens of Antrim? How do you describe them? The Glens (also known as the Antrim Mountains) consist of nine glens – Glentaisie, Glenshesk, Glendun, Glencorp, Glenaan, Glenballyemon, Glenariff, Glencloy and Glenarm. The Glens of Antrim are so much more than places of outstanding beauty – they are a deeply intriguing monument to rural life, full of Irish folklore and stories of giants and fairies. Stretching from the Antrim Plateau to the Causeway Coast, the Glens of Antrim consist of a richly varied landscape of impressive valleys, thickly wooded glens and outstanding waterfalls. Three of the more well known waterfalls are located in Glenariff, the Ess-na-Larach, Ess-na-Crub and Mare's Tail, the latter dropping hundreds of feet down the side of the glen. However, there are plenty of lesser known falls dotted throughout the Glens for those willing to get off the beaten track.

The most well known and beautiful forest park in the Glens of Antrim is Glenariff Forest, located on the main Ballymena to Waterfoot road. As well as providing a variety of walks, you also have splendid views down through Glenariff Glen towards the village of Waterfoot. On a clear day, you can see Scotland from here.

Another popular yet intriguing area is Loughareema, also known to the locals as 'The Vanishing Lake'. A strange phenomenon where one day the lake can be full, and the next it can be bone dry. Following a tragedy there in 1898 when a colonel, coachman and two horses all drowned, rumours now abound that a ghostly horse and carriage inhabit the area…

As a photographer, it is always a challenge to capture a scene at its best. For this, you need the right light. But this is what this book is all about. To showcase the beauty that we are fortunate to have, right on our own doorstep. The Glens of Antrim and the surrounding Antrim Plateau provide a vast range of photographic material – this book is my take on some of my favourite locations and viewpoints.

ACKNOWLEDGEMENTS

First and foremost, I'd like to thank my wife Lynne, for her continued love, support and encouragement. Without that, this book would never have been completed.

I'd also like to thank Steven Pugsley and the team at Halsgrove Publishing for taking the vision for this book onboard and running with it. I appreciate all the hard work that has gone into designing, editing and printing this book. It has been a privilege to work with so many talented and enthusiastic people.

4

Snow always transforms the landscape. This is an old homestead close to Slemish mountain on the Antrim Plateau.

Early morning light skips across the fields close to Slemish mountain.

There are many of these old ruined houses dotted across the Antrim Plateau, hinting at life hundreds of years ago. This one is on the side of Skerry Hill, close to Slievenamaddy.

Glenariff, which many consider to be the most picturesque of all the Glens. This is the view looking down the Glen towards the tiny coastal village of Waterfoot.

Overleaf:
Autumn colours in Glenarm Forest.

This is close to Bryvore Bridge, on the approach to Glendun and Glenaan.

Loughareema, also known as the 'Vanishing Lake'. One day you'll find it full of water, the next it could be empty...

Slemish mountain after
a very heavy snowfall.

Early morning mist and frost.

Glendun. What a wonderful site to call 'home', nestled close to Glendun Viaduct.

Overleaf:
The drive between Glendun and Ballycastle can provide some fantastic views looking back across the Glens towards Glenballyemon and Glenariff.

Early morning light over Glenarm Glen, with Slemish mountain just about visible in the distance.

The approach to
Glenarm Glen.

Glenarm Glen on a beautiful midsummer's morning.

The view looking back
over to Glenarm Forest.

A common feature of Glenarm Glen is the quaint little stone walls separating one field from another.

Lovely warm morning light hits this lone tree in Glenarm Glen.

Looking down Glenballyemon
towards Gaults Road.

Overleaf:
Glenballyemon and
Tievebulliagh.

Low cloud on the hills
looking towards Trostan.

Early morning light looking up Glendun, taken from the Glendun Viaduct.

Ess-na-Crub Waterfall,
Glenariff Forest Park.

When water levels are quite low, it is possible to get right up to the face of the Ess-na-Crub Waterfall in Glenariff Forest Park.

The view looking down
the Glenariff River.

One of the beautiful forest
paths within Glenariff Forest.

Another waterfall, this one just beside the Rainbow Bridge, in Glenariff Forest.

Close-up of the
Glenariff River.

The view looking from
Waterfoot beach
towards Lurigethan.

The magnificent Lurigethan
and Glenariff Glen.

Overleaf:
Glencorp.

Glencorp, and the chapel in Cushendall.

The view looking towards Glencorp, Glenaan and Glendun.

This is the view from the side of Lurigethan looking over towards Tievebulliagh and Glenaan.

The front face of Lurigethan.

Green fields, blue skies
and fluffy white clouds...
This combination is
sometimes a rarity
in Northern Ireland.

Many areas in the Glens can be quite desolate and bare, yet still beautiful...

Overleaf:
The other side of Lurigethan
from the Gaults Road.

Glencorp, looking towards
Glenaan and Tievebulliagh.

Glencorp.

High up on Glenaan, the views are fantastic.

One of the most picturesque
of all the Glens, Glendun, is
home to the Glendun Viaduct.

Part of the Moyle Way,
and Slieveanorra Forest
in the distance.

Slieveanorra Forest with
Orra More in the distance.

The Antrim Plateau is full of vibrant contrasting colours, as shown here.

En-route to Glenariff from Cargan, you will come across this old stone 'house' almost at the side of the road.

Deep snow in Glenariff Forest.

The great view you have looking down Glenariff Glen.

You can clearly see from here the U-shaped Glen of Glenariff which was shaped this way in the Ice Age.

Overleaf:
Looking over to Slievenanee and Trostan.

The side face of Glenariff,
Queen of the Glens.

Early morning light catches the bluebells in full bloom.

The wind turbines situated on
Slievenahanaghan.

Glentaisie on a summer's evening.

Evening light through Glentaisie.

Morning light on Glencorp.

Overleaf:
Amazing views looking down
to Lurigethan and Glenariff.

Popular features of the Glens are the forest parks with their vast displays of bluebells.

Evening light catches the blue-bells in Glenariff Forest.

The Glendun River, which runs down through the heart of Glendun.

The Ess-na-Crub Waterfall in
Glenariff Forest is definitely
one of the gems of the whole
Glens of Antrim.

A waterfall in the
Glenariff River.

Morning light on the Antrim
Plateau, close to Cargan.

Part of the Antrim Plateau, this section is just off the main Ballymena to Waterfoot road.

In summer, the old stone
house is almost hidden
by the leaves of the tree.

Overleaf:
If you rise early in the
morning, you quite often
have places like this
all to yourself.

A striking contrast between the colours of the Glen and the bright yellow of the digger.

Looking towards
Glendun and Glencorp.

The Torr Road takes you out of Cushendun, and provides you with superb views looking back down onto the village.

Looking towards
Glenariff Forest Park.

Looking to Glenariff Forest Park and Craignamaddy.